Golden Leaves

James Stephen Christian

authorHOUSE®

AuthorHouse™
1663 Liberty Drive
Bloomington, IN 47403
www.authorhouse.com
Phone: 833-262-8899

Published by AuthorHouse 08/11/2022

ISBN: 978-1-6655-6842-5 (sc)
ISBN: 978-1-6655-6841-8 (e)

Print information available on the last page.

CONTENTS

ABOUT THE AUTHOR

James Stephen Christian, born April 10, 1956 in Detroit, Michigan.

I began writing when I was twenty.

I've lived in Michigan, Colorado, and Hawaii.

I have a large family.

My parents - James Walter and Margaret Mary.

Siblings - Artus, Michele, Nicolette, Mark, and Robyn.

Children - Kyle James, Joli Michelle, Shane Michael, Robert James, Garret Gabriel and granddaughter Emersyn Joli.

APRIL SON

Here the old world is a gift from me,
    To God and humanity
        I offer my Golden Leaves of poetry.
Thoughts of passion and spirit
    Expressing the essence of me.

Myself, Jamie
    The life, light, and shadow of a man.
My character is one of an athlete, adventurer, comic, music lover,
    Poet, beachcomber, stargazer, and Christian.
I am a young man who has old dreams.

In my mind, there's the peace and anguish of daily living.
In my dreams, there's optimism.
In my body, there's strength.
In my heart, there's love.
In my spirit, there's the desire for adventure.

I feel old,
    As though my life has always been.
I feel young,
    With my April birth, spring begins.
I believe tomorrow holds the future
    For one as young as I am.

Chapter 1

A GALLERY OF STARS

A gallery of stars
    Blazing wildly throughout the centuries.
A watery, earthly planet
    Floating amid this bountiful universe,
        Shrouded in mystery.

Then man appears
    Sailing ships.
Ships upon the sea
    And across the sky.
Past and present
    Mankind keeps searching,
        Searching for the reasons why?

AS THE YEARS CHANGE

As the year's change one's mind
  My present dreams are even better
    Than the ones I left behind!

BEGINNING MY BOOK

Now that I have little but pen and paper
    It's a good time for me to start writing.
Words come to mind rich and true
    Leaving a sincere meaning.

CLOSING MY EYES

Closing my eyes, I can dream
    Of many splendorous scenes.
But the reality of a simple touch
    Is more significant than all of my dreams.

DECEMBER LEAVES

The autumn winds twirled thousands upon thousands of leaves tumbling
    over a large grassy field.
As I sat against a tree one afternoon, I imagined a historic battlefield.
Those leaves represented to me the men from the north and south.
The fathers and sons who once lived in peace
    Then were scattered in the changing winds.
A man's fear shouted the battle cries during the war as a bayonet ripped
    one's guts out.
Vast armies clashed with swords, rifles, and cannons, slaughtering each
    other.
They burned down towns and devastated the countryside.

It was a shame, men having died in bitter agony.
The once-proud heritages of those nameless corpses lay silent, piled on top
    of one another.
One's blood ran down, mixing with one's enemy.
Failure to love had poured out hate from large open wounds.
The countless ghost soldiers could hear no taps.
A late autumn wind cast brown leaves passing over massive, unmarked
    graveyards.
There was no glory written on the faces of the dead soldiers
    Their eyes portrayed shock; open mouths seemed to be asking why?

The Lord Jesus was busy working between the trenches on both sides
    during the killing,
    Saving souls in no man's land.
Answering prayers that scared men spoke who knew they were about
    to die.

A young woman shed tears like soft summer rain.
She promised her lover she would wait for his return,
But now, his body is laid to rest beneath the swaying shade of the
weeping willow where they first met.
She took a ribbon from her hair, tying it to a bough blowing in the air,
which floated his soul away.
She then bowed to say a silent prayer.

We fought this war on our native land.
Our forefathers waged war against their fellow citizens in the front yards
of their homes.
While their families waved goodbye, wailing from the porches.
The women gander at the wintry trees standing with their dark branches
left bare,
"Our menfolk will never be home in time for Christmas."

Once the skies were blue, then they turned gray
As gravediggers continued planting dead bodies
That fell from the divided flags of America.
All the December Leaves lie dead and frozen, buried beneath the soil they
once lived.
It was such an epic tragedy that we didn't abolish slavery and preserve the
union on peaceful terms.

ENCHANTING EMBRACE

Spring smelled so fresh.
I stared at her as she flowered into summer.
So beautiful had my Lady Spring become
    That I knew I would cherish the memory of her.

When next she changed color, I thought how unpredictable Spring
    could be,
    Yet more radiant than ever.
I held her in my arms.
    But she didn't stay that autumn way either.

Sadly, to my dismay, Spring fell.
She just died there, frozen in my arms like winter.

After a while, though, she came back to life.
She was my Spring again,
    Blossoming all around me, praise be.
I came to realize that Lady Spring lives on forever,
    She, just like a woman, changes her color now and again.

HAWAIIAN NIGHTS

Hawaiian nights are balmy, full of harmony.
I love sitting on the beach.
    Overlooking the midnight-blue ocean,
        Breathing in a warm tropical breeze.
Coconut palms wave as the tide rushes in.
A crescent moon dips toward the west.
Drums beat in the background from hula-show lit by torches.
A few tourists pass by.
A boat bell clangs in the black distance.

Nighttime, to dwell here.
The ocean waves ever so consoling.
The stars are glistening softly.
Suddenly a light flashes, streaking the night sky.
A shooting star,
    Descending from afar.
Stars, seas of distant tears,
    Glowing drops of light.
For tranquility, I vision beauty,
    Of beauty, I vision myself alone with God,
        And the heavens.

HUMBLY YOURS

I am but a poet
    Whose thoughts dwell among the flowers.
With only my love to offer you
    For all the hours.

MEMORIES, FOND MEMORIES

Memories, fond memories return to my mind and heart sometimes
    When I'm quiet, at ease, walking through nature looking her loveliest.
Then I wish that those memories were within my eyesight,
    My arms reach like before, once more.

MISSING IN ACTION

He laid his head down on a bed of leaves, planted like a seed in a jungle
of Vietnam.
He was a Green Beret, mortally wounded, and separated from his team.
Memories flashed within his mind.
He once felt that his life span would never end.

Thinking about his fate as his heartbeat grew faint, his eyes became one
with the heavens.
The night appeared to be a boundless ocean of stars.
Trying to kneel, moonlight on his camouflaged painted face and a spot
of darkness within,
Praying hands caught falling tears.
He had faith he believed would save his soul.
Now there were angels above waiting for him.

As he died in his arms, the plants buried over him a long way from home.
The fiery stars were his last sight.
His spirit ascended with Godspeed toward those temple lights to meet his
Maker.
In the wind, you could hear a whisper.
I was, I am, I will never be,
As I once thought of myself.

MORNING WINGS

Morning brings another day,
    Another breath of life.
A new awakening,
    And another chance at life!

MY CHILD, MY LIFE

My child, my life,
May you be a child of Light from birth.
May your dreams be of beauty.
May your way be one of caring and giving.
May your hands be helpful, working.
May your eyes be set on justice.
May your mind be at peace, full of understanding.
May compassion sing about your heart, forgiving.
May your soul be free and contented.
May your thoughts be creative, exploring the supremeness of love which
    is unending.
May you worship God and obey Him.
May your smile always be youthful.
May you find wisdom in humility.
May you attain the joys life has to offer and overcome its sorrows.
My child, my life,
May you always remember my love for you.

NIGHT LIGHT

The morning sun rose without a whisper.
Daylight passed once again the way time always does.
The moon now can be seen dwelling among the heavens,
   Quietly passing beneath the stars this night, similar to other nights.
Beneath these stars burned a candle-flame
   Set beside me as I spent a creative evening.
There was solitude in the air as I pondered over my written words.

Many books lie on the shelves having no voice of their own.
Often I sit at my desk deep in thought
   Writing and typing for hours and hours unending.
When my soul ascends into eternity
   I hope people will have found my words to be noteworthy.

With prayers echoing in my head,
   I looked out the window from my bed.
The constellations portray a celestial kingdom.
The moon appeared to be staring down at me.
I love its sentimental light,
   The way it vividly gleams throughout the night.
As I drift off to sleep, I am determined to thrive.
My head radiates with the brilliance of being alive.

NORTH SHORE OF OAHU

Morning clouds billow and gust across the sky,
 Gigantic whitecap waves roll in and by.
Standing alone as though on top of the world
 The wind, sand, and sea become me.
I am just a spirit on the roam,
 Free to be with no place to call home.
Father Spirit, I know You hear me,
 Lead me; lead me by the hand,
  My footprints in the sand.

POETRY

Sunlight peered through a window onto a desktop.
A dusty room filled with books.
A blank sheet of paper issued a challenge,
    So many possibilities.
What could be said?
What needs to be said?
The deepest thoughts can be too deep
    To ever surface.

To have a life of simplicity and turn it into one of creativity.
Poetry is cheerful; it's a dirge.
Often personal, yet read by others.
Timeless, yet watching the hours.

SKY BIRDS

The midday sun rays felt hot and soothing.
My brother and I were leaning back against some driftwood
    On a beach in Key West sightseeing.
Laughing gulls circled above, looking at ease
    Gliding aloft a breeze.

I love the way the seagulls fly,
    Casting their wings filled with light against the blue sky
     Like white sails gusting by.
Airborne over the waterway
    They kiss the wind good day.

SLEEPLESS NIGHT

'Twas a starry, starry night
    And in my eyes could be seen both the darkness and light.
Thoughts about all I lost
    And the things I might never reap.
It made me toss,
    I could not fall asleep.

SPRING AIR

It was a time in spring,
    A time when nature is uplifting.
When birds are aloft on the wing
    And children play on a swing.
When the scenery is colorful
    From leaves and lilacs blooming, this is spring!

THE MEADOW

The meadow is pristine, bright, and spacious
 But I live in the ghetto
  And have never seen the meadow.

THE MOON ALSO SETS

The sun's golden rays fell upon a small stone house
    Resting on a hilltop covered with tropical plants.
Sunshine passing through stained glass
    Danced a spectrum of colors in a den.
An open window admitted a warm breeze,
    Turning over the pages of a notebook echoing with fresh thoughts.
The compiling of a book lay in a stack of typed papers
    Set to the side of an oak desk.
Gardenias placed in a gold-leaf vase perfumed the air.
A cardinal flew on the windowsill,
    Leaping on the desktop, he pecked at a handful of seeds placed there
        for one such as he.
Music was playing on the stereo.

My imagination is lively, like the surf tossed around this endless summer
    island.
Strolling toward the window with a melody lingering,
    It framed a serene picture of the skyline over the ocean.
Orange cloud puffs were floating in the west.
Snacking on grapes and cashews
    I recalled how earlier, God painted a dazzling rainbow archway.

Going out onto the balcony,
    Anxious to watch the sunset,
        Clouds blew in the way.
Wondering, wondering
    Was the sun ever meant to set this way?
I imagined the lost horizon to be a massive fireball boiling the surface.
Morning is awakening half a world away.
High above, the moon is sailing on its voyage over the darkening sky,
    Slowly trailing the sun.
The full moon resembled a giant pendulum
    Swinging among the twilight stars.

Settling in a rocking chair, I lit a lantern,
    And drank a margarita.
The night's trade winds reminded me of an old song
    As I relaxed.
Twilight is a quiet time,
    Much too romantic to be spent alone,
        All the stars sparkle like a throne.

The evening sky grew dark, starry dark.
In time I realized
    The moon also sets.
        Casting its reflection glittering off the water
           As it continued to sink below the black ocean
Moonbeams and dreams are splendorous things
I sense the Salvation Cross setting
    And the Son is rising!

THE MUSIC OF LIFE

The music of life,
    Where does it go after one's body turns cold?

Where is that smile, that friend,
    That sister who I use to know?

THE STAR IN ME

The star in me.
Sometimes I fantasize, dwelling a world away from reality.
I am a star in my dreams.
Even though, in reality, things are not quite that bright.
But a dream would not be a dream
    If it did not have a star.
And I could not be happy today
    If I did not dream of tomorrow
        And believe!

TIME BURIED IN ETERNITY

Time is buried in eternity.
The minutes pass into hours,
    Hours into days,
        Days into weeks,
            And weeks into months.
As the seasons change into years,
    Ticking by like the seconds of a clock.

Time runs out like sand pouring through a broken hourglass
    Blowing in eternity.
There time ends,
    And infinity continues.

TONIGHT WILL BRING TOMORROW

Tonight will bring tomorrow.
Tomorrow arrives today.
Yesterday was a day like tomorrow,
    Which we allowed slip away.

VOYAGE OF THE GHOST SHIP P.1

It was a stormy night, lost at sea.
Our ship, near wrecked, had been blown far off its course by a hurricane.
Howling winds tore at the rigging while huge waves crashed against the
    hull,
    Tossing the ship around like a speck of wood.
Pitch-black clouds covered the heavens as thunder stormed.

"Captain, Captain!" I shouted.
"We have struck a reef; we are taking in water on the starboard side!"
This vessel's voyage had ended abruptly as its sails disappeared beneath a
    turbulent sea.
We lost all hands.

Reborn, never to live again.
Outer space, where ghost ships sail endlessly.
Countless stars sparkled throughout the dense solitude.
The stars appeared to be radiant pearls cast in an ocean of motion.
The masts were raging, ablaze with energy that sped us onward.
Our ship rocketed across the solar system like a shooting comet.
Strange light forms surrounded us,
    Similar to gulls and dolphins.
These creatures acted as though they wanted to guide us,
    But where?

"Captain, some of the men are experiencing a reoccurring nightmare
    Of drowning trapped aboard the flooded ship."
"Lieutenant, summon the men on deck; I shall address the ship's company."
"Aye, aye, sir."

"Men, be not fearful like pilgrims lost in a snow blizzard.
We are seamen, be brave!
I lost control of my ship because nature overwhelmed me.
We men who sought adventure now have an opportunity to search the lost
    frontiers of our souls
    Before our bodies had a chance to grow old.
We are past the grave now; our journey is like no other.
Regain your dignity, and let us sail for liberty!
Lieutenant, men, hoist up the flag,
    Fire the cannons in a salute to the glory of this quest,
        And set sail toward the northern galaxy."
"Aye, aye, sir."
"I shall find land, enough to bury the past!"

VOYAGE OF THE GHOST SHIP P.2

The men took to heart our Captain's message.

His optimism and discipline inspired us to work harder than ever to
serve him

In the hope of discovering a fertile planet.

His eyes became shark-like,

Staring out to space as he stood at the helm.

Anyone could tell he was determined to thrive.

We wandered and wandered for light-years

Until we became like driftwood.

Finally, a shout from the crow's nest called out: "Ahoy, land ahead!"

We spotted a planet, so we began orbiting it.

The men all yelled: "Hooray, hooray!"

But the Captain just bowed his head.

Landing on the planet, we found it to be nothing but sand.

Tumbleweeds rustled against the bow as we went cruising along on a sea
of sand,

Rudder bone-dry, scratching the barren surface.

The Captain turned into a phantom astronomer,

He is spending most of his time in his cabin drawing navigational
charts.

Knocking on his door, I entered and saw him standing there,

Blindly staring out a bay window at a crimson sky.

A harsh stone-faced moon was rolling by.

He paid me no heed.

He held a vase of strawflowers in his hand.

It has been twenty light-years since I've last heard him cry,

When we realized that the families we loved had died,

Yet the tears now, as previously, flew from his dark shadowy eyes.

The logbook written in his mind remains a mystery to us all.

"Captain, Captain, what am I to tell the crew?
They have lost hope in this deserted desert.
What are we supposed to do now, sir?"
"Lieutenant, you're a good lad; you must believe there is hope.
Set sail out of here in a northeast direction."
"Aye, aye, sir."
"Lad, every sailor among us chose the sea as a way of life
    By placing their backbones firmly on the deck.
Now our backs have broken under great stress.
However, be it on sea, space, or sand, a ship must stay afloat.
To live on the sea, we must sail by the stars.
Where there is life, there will always be a new birth."

WATCHING THE RIVER FLOW

Waking in the morning
    I felt anxious to be outdoors.
Not having anywhere to go,
    I went down to watch the river flow.
Once there, it felt good to relax among the golden Aspen trees
    And not worry about anything.

A breeze rustled the leaves,
    As the moon rolled over the Colorado Rockies.
I thought about how the past is but a memory.
The future but a dream,
    And the present is just the way things are.
Savoring this carefree spell
    My eyes followed the ripples on the clear water.

WHERE ARE THE CLOUDS

Where are the clouds?
The sky is clear, but I feel blue,
    There ought to be a cloud or two.
Wind, send in the clouds.

WITH AUTUMN

With autumn, the summer leaves fell
    And blew towards winter.
I wished that it be spring again
    But no, only rain came, followed by snow.

Chapter 2

AN ARTIST'S EYES

An artist's eyes see the drama of the world in colors,
  Colors fulfilling the seasons.
Art is inspired by a flowery summer,
    Falling into memorable autumn,
      Freezing into a starving winter,
        Melting into a rainy spring's wind of humility.
Moods motivate the movements of one's hands.
Tears reveal the personal work of one's sentimental years.

An artist is a gifted person who further develops their skill through
  experience.
One ardently strives for perfection,
  expressing themselves through creating an image.
Leonardo dreamed, and "The Last Supper" was seen.
Michelangelo suffered, and "The Pieta" was brought to life.
Rembrandt fell in love and portrayed Jesus' face.
The masters have filled the Vatican and museums with paintings and
  sculptures
holding the ages of history.

BEAUTY IN JESUS

Beauty in Jesus blessing the children.
Jesus is a man of joys and sorrows.
Christ dying on the cross,
    Our Savior's blood raining upon us.
The skies grew dark as night.
Beauty in his eyes,
    Eyes that no longer had sight.

Beauty in the virgin birth,
    In a Spiritual anointing,
        A sermon on the mount.

Beauty in a man's love for God and humanity.
Blood poured out from nail wounds piercing his hands and feet.
Beauty in a compassionate face
    Now bloody, tearful.
A mock crown of thorns piercing his mind anguished,
    This High Priest of Peace.

Beauty in Jesus, by His stripes, we are made whole, complete.
A spear sprung forth water and blood from his side,
    Water spirit, blood earth.
The Son of God became flesh and walked among us.
The truth was told by one who didn't have a chance to grow old.
Beauty in a man who willingly sacrificed his life
    So that others may live.

Beauty in a Father's love,
    In a Resurrection!
O to take the hardest of circumstances
    And turn them into something glorious.
Beauty in Jesus the Christ!

BEDTIME THOUGHTS

Dear God, I hope You had a great day
    Making dreams come true for those who pray.
God lives out His dreams
    Through people who pray.
Pray, pray every day.

HOLY LIFE

There is life!
Where there is life, there is no death,
    Holy Life.

LAST NIGHT

Last night I asked God for everything,
I wanted everything,
All He had.
I asked Him for His love.

SAINT PAUL, CHRISTIAN

Saint Paul was a sailor,
   Pioneering Christianity.
He was a prisoner,
   Who wrote in the darkness of a dungeon
      About the Greatest Light the world has ever known.
Apostle Paul's faith set his soul free,
   Sailing in Heaven's glory!

THE STARS

The stars, the stars have always been there
    And yet my immortal soul
        Will outlast their flare.

Chapter 3

A BABY'S FIRST TOOTH

A baby's first tooth,
    Sweet.
But O, how I miss that gummy smile!

DREAMS OF TOMORROW

A boy building a sandcastle,
  A knight on a distant quest.
Children are the dreams of tomorrow.

MY LITTLE MAN AND ME

My little man and me
    Walking along the windy sea.
Without him, no matter what I had
    It would not be enough.

A WINTER'S NIGHT

'Twas a winter's night,
    Fresh snow made the city appear pure.
A northern wind broke the silence hovering over the atmosphere.
The snowy moon rose among the stars glistening like icicles.
Christmas just passed,
    The year 2000 approaches.
But no sleigh bells can be heard passing through the city streets.
There used to be sleigh-bells ringing.

BEAUTIFUL GLOW

I don't think you'll ever know
how much I love you.
How dark the place
when at first I saw you,
    Your face.
You are such a Beautiful Glow.

BEAUTY IN THE NIGHT

Beauty in the night, my beautiful wife.
Her angelic face,
    Caribbean eyes,
        Pink kissable lips, wild tongue,
           And flowing golden hair.
I embrace her nakedness as she cuddles beside me.
Her body is smooth, shapely, and warm.
My wife passionately loves me.
Making music at night.

CHILD

Child, there is so much for you to learn,
    So much for you to be.
Life at times is a haunting mystery,
    A pleasurable paradise,
        And a gray void in between the extremes.
Life is a gamble,
    But it's a chance worth taking.
So welcome into the world, my child.

I HAD YOU

I had you,
    Your face, lips, and tongue.
Your breast,
    Body and toes.

I had you,
    Your touch.
Your warmth and passion,
    You, my Lover.

IF I CAN HOLD YOU

If I can hold you,
    Squeeze you
        And bite you?
Make you scream
    Then I know that you are real
        I'm not in a dream.

LIFE IS GOOD

The beauty of nature,
Sun by day, moon and stars by night.
Wind through a willow reminds me of a woman's hair
Hanging long and flowing.
The sound a ripple makes in the water.
A white seagull against the blue-sky.
Seasons changing.
Children growing.
A gray, rainy afternoon.
The aroma of bread baking.
The sweet deliciousness of fruit.
Family together for dinner,
Laughter, smiles, and more laughter.
Small things that mean so much.

LIVING FOR THE MOMENTS

Living for the moments,
    Passion! Passion!
Moments of passion,
    Here then spent.
I'm living for the moments,
    Living for the moments.

O, WHAT A FEELING

O, what a feeling, what a feeling,
it's true;
    Nowhere I'd rather be than here with you.
I see your face,
    And want to embrace everything that you are.

O, what a feeling, what a feeling,
it's true;
    Nowhere I'd rather be than here with you.
No one I'd rather do than you.

O, what a feeling, what a feeling,
it's true;
    Nowhere I'd rather be than here with you.
I love you,
    Love you,
        You.

OCEANSIDE

Oceanside,
   A summer's day.
Her eyes were like the bay,
   Looks like the bay.

REFLECTIONS AND SHADES

Reflections, reflections of dreams, beautiful dreams pass and present
    Appeared to one while he stood on a cliff overlooking the surf.
The wind swelled like waves splashing against his face,
    Gulls cried out in mid-flight.
Sometimes it's best not to want more out of a dream
    Then simply the dream itself.
He was a loner who beheld the stately clouds
    And wanted to drift.
As the day passed
    His vision flared from a purple sky, pink clouds, and a yellow sunset
        Among an orange ocean.
Soon his thoughts changed into these hues
    Then a misty rain began to fall.

SANDPIPERS

Ormond Beach, Florida, grassy dunes, sea turtle nests
    And the call of sandpipers at play.
It feels good to take a timeout and watch them running along the seashore
    on a sunny, windy day.

Taking in the afternoon sun
    I'm feeling the Atlantic Ocean's tide rush in across my feet.
I wish I could hold time and not let go of this golden moment
    Having my lovely wife and son around me.

Come evening it's where do you want to go for dinner?
Then like the sunset, we're gone.

SCHOOL DAYS

I'll wait for you,
    And watch the seasons change.
I'll wait for you,
    And watch you grow taller each year.

I'll wait for you,
    And watch you come walking across the grass
        With the sunlight in your hair.
I'll wait for you,
    Each day and know that I will miss this precious time
        When you no longer come.

I'll wait for you,
    Even though I know that you won't wait for me
        Because you have to move on
            And I can't.

STAY WITH ME NOW

Stay with me now,
    I love you with my whole heart and soul,
        And need you even more.
Stay with me now,
    Be mine forevermore!

THE DAYS OF LOVING YOU

The days of loving you are the best days
    Through and through.
I can never get enough,
    It always feels like the first time.
Being with you is sublime.

THE MIND HAS A MILLION DREAMS

The mind has a million dreams,
    But the heart just one.
The dream of love.

TORONTO

Dining with my family one evening in a classic restaurant
　　I saw a painting hanging on the wall.
It depicted an era of nearly a hundred years ago,
　　A time now long gone passed.
Families ice skating outdoors on the frozen canals,
　　Boys playing shinny hockey on the fly.
All those bright shining faces that once were
　　And are no more.

WE WERE YOUNG LOVERS

We were young lovers,
    One summer.
One special summer,
    One flaming ember.

YOUR SMILE

In the light of day,
    I see your eyes, your lips.
In the light of day,
    Beyond gorgeous, I see your face.

Looking at your face,
    I thought what a stunning beauty you are.
Then you smiled,
    Suddenly there were no words
        Just sheer radiance!

YOU'RE BEAUTIFUL, BEAUTIFUL

You're beautiful, beautiful,
   Through and through.
I love and adore you.

You're beautiful, beautiful,
   Through and through.
I want you.

You're beautiful, beautiful,
   Through and through.
I need you.

COLORS FADED TO GRAY

A rosy face
    Hidden by shadows.
A blood-red heart
    Lost in loneliness.
Colors,
    Faded to gray.

COME TO ME IN THE SPRING

Come to me in the spring,
    When all the trees and flowers are blossoming,
        Birds singing,
            And the grass growing.

Come to me in the spring,
    My Love,
        When life appears everlasting!

DO YOU LOVE ME

Do you love me?
    If you say yes
        I will love you in a thousand ways.

Do you love me?
    If you say yes
        We'll always be together.

Do you love me?
    If you say yes
        If only you would say yes.

Do you love me?
    Say yes!

GARRET GABRIEL

I love you, son,
　　Love you so.
I thank God for you
　　Your sweet soul.

You loved me
　　When I needed someone
　　　　You were there until the day was done.

You loved me,
　　Loved me so.
I thank God for you,
　　And will never let you go.

You have my heart,
　　You're all the joy therein
　　　　My dear friend.

I COME TO YOU

I come to you lying in a field of glory.
A sunny, grassy meadow of wildflowers,
    Birds singing and willows swaying.

I come to you lying in a field.
A spirit rushing over you,
    Your splendor.

I come to you lying in a field
    Of daydreams
        Full of passion.

I come to you lying in a field
    Alone with great anticipation.
Eyes wide open,
    Mouth hungering.
O, to love someone lost
    Then found.
How great the treasure.

I come to you lying in a field
    With tall grass as a pillow.
Spirit of love upon you,
    You are an ever-flowing river of song and music.
O, heavenly lady,
    Sweet bride of mine.

I LOVE YOU FROM AFAR

I love you from afar,
   As one would wish upon a star.

I LOVE YOU

I love you,
I love you on a spring's day,
    And in a summer's way.
I love you in every way.

I love you,
I love your face,
    And see it everyplace.
On a fall afternoon,
    And on a winter's moon.

I love you,
I see you and pray
    That you will not look away
        But love me in the same way.

IT RAINED TODAY

It rained today,
    Outside the windowpane, the rain is pooling.
I don't know what will be tomorrow
    But it rained today.
In some distant places, the sun is shining
    But here it rained today.

JOLI

There was a little girl I knew
     She turned out to be so blue.
This little girl I knew.

If only I could undo
     That which has made her so blue.
Restoring her spirit anew.
Know that I, your father, love you.

LONELINESS HOLDS NO EMBRACE

Loneliness
holds no embrace.

LONELY LOOKING SKY

Lonely-looking sky,
    Lonely sky.
All my days,
    Dreams that have gone by,
Lonely looking sky.

LOOKING OUT TO SEA

Looking out to sea with uncertainty,
    The undulating sea.
What do I see?
Searching God for answers,
    Thoughts become me.

MUSIC, POETRY, AND PRAYER

Music, poetry, and prayer.
My days are easy now.
It's a morning in May.
Walking to Lake St. Clair,
the scent of lilacs is in the air.
Once there, the blue sea and sky caught my eye,
meditating in prayer.

OCEANS CRASH BEFORE ME

Oceans crash before me,
 I've lost my wife.
Oceans crash before me
 My love is gone as I knew it in my life.

'Twas the autumn of my life,
 Everything changing, colorful but dying.
Now that it is the end,
 I find myself thinking about the beginning.

That girl I loved became my wife.
The children she bore, we brought it to life.

Memories of the moments of love,
 The love we shared.
Moments of a love that was
 But they are no more.

What once meant so much,
 A photograph, a memory, one's birthday.
Now it's over, and all the meaning has changed.
Life can be so strange.

The world turns, and time passes away.
Things that mattered fade to gray.

I miss you; I miss us
 What was, what could have been.
If only the love we shared would have lasted.
Last and last,
 If only.
Wondering, wondering
 Will I ever see the ocean again?

REACHING OUT

Having suffered loss, a significant loss.
    I find myself reaching,
        Reaching out.
Reaching,
    Still reaching,
        Ever reaching.

REGRETS

It's a hard rain that's falling,
    It's a hard rain that has fallen on me.
I feel so much pain,
    It's a hard rain.

SMILE, I LOVED YOUR SMILE

Smile, I loved your smile,
   That dimpled smile.
Whatever happened to that smile,
   Your smile that used to smile at me?

SUMMER JOY

The butterflies look joyful,
   Even though they're only here for a season.
They don't worry about it
   Because they're living for the season,
      They're living for the season!

THE CLOUDS OF YESTERYEAR

Watching a western movie,
    Beholding the sky in the background
        And the clouds of yesteryear.
Thinking about
    Days gone by that were once here.
Lives that lived before
    And are no more.
O, how I miss
    The clouds of yesteryear.

THE COLORS OF MY LIFE

The colors of my life,
   Colors, like stars and scars, they're all here.
The colors of my life,
   Colors I bore and have to accept.
The colors of my life,
   They're all here, everywhere.

THE DAY IS THROUGH

Midnight's majestic skyline.
The dark ocean surges
as the world turn to recline.
Moonlight glows through the clouds
onto the deep.
My thoughts,
thoughts before sleep?
Are of you,
    You.

THE MONARCHS RETURNED

Autumn falls around me,
    Looking out from the water's edge
        Out over the lake toward the lighthouse where we once and she
            still lives.
Last summer we were together
    But no longer.

Summer will come again,
    The monarchs will return to the purple butterfly bush
        That they're so fond of
            But what happened to her, to us?

TO LOVE AGAIN

Facing inner struggles
    Day after morning day.
Hoping for that which is sublime
    Time after time.

I can pray walking through a winter's sunny midday.
I can write poetry that's positive or astray
    But when will I ever meet her?
When will I ever meet her anyway?

The evening is fading, fading away,
    Blue-skies turning gray
Passing through shadows,
    Lamenting lost.
I am just someone the world doesn't see,
    God have mercy and set my soul free.

Seeing the Light,
    The Light of a new life, a new world dawning.
Rediscovering a hidden truth,
    I'll learn to love again.
I'll fall in love,
    Deeply in love with someone new.

Take my hand,
    Take this walk down life's roadways,
        A way with me.
See what we may see,
    Be all we can dream of being.
Love is free,
    My love for you will always be,
        Love me.

WAVES

Like waves reaching the shore,
    The days keep splashing against my face.
Reminding me of another time,
    Another place.

WHEN AT FIRST YOU LOVED ME

When at first you loved me,
    You had to be with me.
For years,
    You had to be with me.

Now breaking up is easy for you,
    You want to be free.
But not for me,
    I miss you.
I miss the one, who had to be with me,
    When at first you loved me.

WHIRLWIND

I am wild; people can't understand me,
    My wild ways.
It's who I am, what I am.
A wild spirited man,
    Believing in a quest.
Living like a storm,
    Ragging across the land and sea
        Wild me!

WISHING YOU WERE NEAR

It's a rainy night here,
    Wishing you were near
        Whispering the words I want to hear.

You whispered one night.
"You do me just right," before we made love that night.
My love, my Dear,
    Wishing you were near.

YOU WERE SO YOUNG

You were so young when we first met.
My thoughts have often been about you,
 Beauty's on my mind.
But the time has come to say goodbye.
Goodbye to you, my Love.
I'll cherish the memories,
 Memories of passion are all that are left.
You are gone, lost.
Lost in an eternity, moving on.
Goodbye, my Love,
 Farewell setting Sun,
  Farewell.

Chapter 6

A SUMMER'S DAY

Children and flowers blend well together.
Watching my son's and granddaughter's smiling faces
    As they run across a grassy park towards a giant jungle gym.
Fun is in the air!
God, what can I say? You created a summer's day.

BEAUTY IN A DIRGE

To lose myself in poetry is to discover a beautiful, enduring thing.
Beauty in one's love.
Sorrow in one's loss.
Beauty in a dirge that says goodbye,
    Goodbye, my Love.

BY THE WATER'S EDGE

DEDICATED TO MY SON
SHANE MICHAEL CHRISTIAN

A boy rollerblading on a sunny day
    Reminds me of one of my sons at play.
Nothing could be more innocent, carefree
    O, how I yearn for yesterday.
I see him everywhere,
    I stop and turn and think of him there.

By the water's edge of Whidbey Island,
    You used to sit playing chords on your guitar,
        Singing lyrics that you wrote.

I miss you so,
    So very much.
You deserved to make mistakes
    And learn to overcome them even the hard way.
I can't bear the fact that fate took you away.
You were and will always be
    A loving man to me.

Like the wind, one's spirit is gone, yet it is here,
    God is everywhere.
Go with God, my son,
    Be ever near.
Buried in your uniform,
    My navy son, forever you'll be.
Standing at your grave-site
    I salute thee.

CRYING OVER THE LOSS

Crying over the loss of a loved one,
 It's okay to cry.
We learn in pain,
 Pain in separation.
Joy in togetherness,
 Sorrow in death.
What it truly means to love, care and miss.
To be thankful for what we had, have
 And trust in God that anyone loss
  Shall be found in time,
   In Him.

DREAMS AND REALITY

Once I was young now, I feel so old.
To be young and in love is great.
Should one lose their love?
One can find another, and love goes on.
In time should one lose that love
    And find it too late to start over
        Then losing a child as well hurts badly.

I awoke in a dark place, broken,
    Battered, shot to pieces, pulverized.
I heard a voice, the voice lied.
False hopes don't help.
I feel confused, searching for answers in all I know.
What I don't know plagues me.
I all but forgot my dreams of a purpose.
Love remains distant if only it would find me,
    If only.

I recognize the face looking back in the mirror
    Though my beard is as gray as it can be.
I can't help but think one my age should be more intelligent.
Where I'm going, only God knows.
My space pains me; I can't bear it.
Still, the sun rises.

EMME

Emme, you're a sweet girl,
   Just like I knew you'd be
      Sweet Emme!

END OF JUNE

Laying out beside the pool,
    Hot sun beating down, feeling good to my bones.
The water is clear and bright.
Honeysuckle shrubs fragrant the air.
It's summer!

FLAG AND CROSS

My navy son,
    Shane Michael,
        I wish I had told you that I loved you more
           And I told you all the time.
The world was brighter, happier with you.

My navy son,
    I love you.
I lay and kiss your headstone, watering the grass with tears.
I miss you.
My Winnie the Pooh boy grew into a big man.
I am proud of you, son.
All that you were are and will be.
I thank you for loving me.
Remembering those big hugs, I felt and feel your love always.
Jesus said: "Blessed are the pure in heart for they shall see God."
I know you are with our Heavenly Father; your faith has saved you.

My navy son,
One cannot know tears of joy until one has screamed tears of sorrow.
The greater the suffering,
    The greater the joy when we meet in the hereafter.
We'll be together again in a blink of an eye, father and son.
In a blink of an eye…

GOODBYE, GOODBYE

Goodbye, goodbye.
These are the hardest words I've ever spoken.
Goodbye, goodbye, my son.
I would give my life for yours in an instant.
I pray why God didn't take me instead.
Twenty years young, my son,
    My big man, my boy,
        My child, my baby.
O, how I wish God would have taken me instead.
It would be easier because I don't want to live without you.

I think I know now how God the Father felt
    About His Son Jesus dying.
It hurts; it rips one's guts out.
You scream, scream one's name out
    And mourn.
Can't sleep; it hurts to wake.

Goodbye, goodbye, my son.
Until we meet and greet, sharing big hugs in Heaven.
Know that your dad loves you.
I love you.

HAT IN HAND

Standing before a grave, hat in hand, head bowed down,
   Life appears black and white.
Love you,
   Miss you, brother.

I SEE THINGS

I see things,
    Things that are no longer there.
I see things,
    Things that once were.
I see things
    And yearn.

I'M HERE WITH YOU NOW

I'm here with you now.
I miss you whenever we're apart.
It's sad, sad to be apart.

I'm here with you now.
You're the joy of my life.
The reason I look forward to tomorrow,
    Tomorrow when we'll be together.

I'm here with you now.
Happy to be together.
I thank God for you, my son, my angel Garret Gabriel.

INSIDE I'M STRUGGLING

Inside I'm struggling,
    It's complicated.
I hear the words spoken,
    I don't understand.
Inside I'm struggling.

What am I to believe?
What am I to do?
I see you,
but I can't reach you.

Along the way, I've been mistaken.
I look for help
but get no relief.

At times I think I know.
Then I'm wrong again; only grief.
Which direction to go?

LOOKING AHEAD TO WHEN

I wear a mask; I play the clown
    But inside, I hurt, I hurt deep down.
My heart needs repair,
    But one goes on fighting the darkness of despair.

Through my travels, pain tends to follow.
I'm hoping for better times, so on I go onto tomorrow.
Knowing all roads lead to the end.
One day I'll look back at my life and say goodbye to a close friend.
Goodbye, I loved you, loved you when.

Believing in new beginnings
    I'm saddened over lost things,
        Lost along the way
            They wait in the hereafter, I pray.

Looking ahead to when
    When all sorrow is forgotten
        And my heart will mend.

LOVING LOST THINGS

One can love, love another all you can,
But when you lose them, they're gone, gone.
Leaving one grief-stricken.
Can't breathe; my head's swooning.

I am like a ghost
Loving lost things.
Living today in the past.

I love You, Father
And seek Your Face.
The things I've lost
These are things that You gave me in the first place.

MISSING YOU

Missing you, the loss of a loved one,
    No matter the years,
the pain never goes away.
It still feels like
it was only yesterday.

MORE THAN I CAN BEAR

More than I can bear,
    Loving and losing
        Hurts more than I can bear.
Pain raining down on me,
    Nothing but pain raining down on me.

Lost, starting over after all these years
    Hurts more than I can bear.
I am broken,
    My heart and spirit have been broken.

There's no happiness
    if living is without love.
Can't feel warmth anymore.

Pain raining down on me,
    Nothing but icy, frigid pain raining down on me
        More than I can bear.

MY HEAD'S A SPIN

I wander around the streets
    as though I were lost.
Going in circles, my head's a spin.
Going in circles places I've been.

I know what I'm looking for
    But it's something out of reach.
Experiencing moments of peace,
    Followed by anxiety.
Having trouble dealing with each.

Going over in the head things I've gained,
    And some things I've lost.
Debating, hurting over the cost.

I wander around the streets
    as though I were lost.
Going in circles, my head's a spin.
Going in circles places I've been.

NOT KNOWING IS THE HARDEST THING

Not knowing is the hardest thing.
But thinking that you know something to be accurate
    And then realizing that you were mistaken is even worse.

SUDDENLY YOUR WORLD CHANGES

Someone knocks on your door.
Or you receive a phone call,
and suddenly, your world changes.
They're gone, they're gone!
Crying out, the cries of a parent who just lost a child
    These are the saddest cries of them all.

'TWAS A LATE AUTUMN RAINY NIGHT

'Twas a late autumn rainy night.
Looking out an upstairs window
    at a street light.
Dark branches were swaying,
    Music was playing.
Rain and leaves blew down
    all-around.
Something, someone was missing.
I sensed a profound loss,
    An emptiness that needed to be found.

Chapter 7

IF I WAS YOUNG AGAIN

If I was young again
    But no.
If I was young again
    I'd say hello.
Hello, to the girl I was too shy to greet,
    The one who looked so sweet.
If I was young again.

IT HURTS TO LOVE

It hurts to love.
The more one loves, the more it hurts.
Nothing lasts in this world.
It hurts to love.

LOOKING OUT THE WINDOW

Looking out the window, I see a birch tree standing its ground
    With the seasons changing all around.
But I love it best when summer's green leaves abound.

MARGARET MARY

God bless my mother, Margaret Mary Barbieri,
    She instilled in me faith in God and our Lord Jesus
        His Scared Heart.
Mom believed in the power of prayer and prayed every day.
She bore six children, four girls, and two boys.
She was an artistic woman, who loved and collected books,
    She introduced me to poetry.
I'd love to hand you a copy of my book, mom.
Your tremendous love has dramatically helped inspire my song.
It's all coming out now in tears,
    All the challenging years.

NOVEMBER WILDFLOWERS

I was only happy
 When together with my wife and children.
Now that I've suffered a second divorce
 And the loss of a second son
  I realize that being older, I'll never be happy again.

I feel sorrow deep down in my soul,
 My scars have scars.
When love is too much to ask for
 And being alone is too hard to bear.

If love is reason enough to live
Is the lack of love sufficient reason to die?
Walking through a cold grassy field
 All the November wildflowers are dead.

PIECES THAT I LOVE

I feel distant from my writings.
Verses I wrote when young,
    Verses when I was older.
But always there are pieces,
    Pieces that I love.

PLAYING THE WING

Waking up, I realized that I had been dreaming about playing ice hockey.
Skating, taking slap shots and scoring goals.
I felt happy; I was having fun with my friends.

REMEMBER ME WITH LAUGHTER

Remember me with laughter,
　　Laughter for all the years after.

REMEMBERING WHEN

Remember when, as a boy, ice hockey was new to me.
My first pair of professional hockey gloves
    The leather smelled so good.
The interest I had when reading poetry for the first time,
    And then writing my first poem.
When the Spirit of God touched my life,
    Suddenly I was Born Again, never to be the same.
When I first laid eyes on the girl
that would become my wife.
When my first child, a son, was born,
    When all my children were born.

In time, one grows older and becomes accustomed to the way things are.
Hockey is something I used to play.
Writing is just what I do.
Now my ex-wife is someone I loved in the past.
And the children no longer are children; they have lives of their own.
So much to learn; prayer will help.
Remembering when, when it all was new
    And how good it felt.

WHEN THE CHILDREN WERE YOUNG

When the children were young
    I'm thankful I couldn't see then
        The pain I feel today.

When the children were young
    Now all my dreams for them have gone,
        Gone away.

When the children were young
    They didn't know that abusing drugs and alcohol
        Would lead their lives astray.

When the children were young
    They were happy,
        Happy at play.

WISDOM

Knowledge plus willpower
   Equals wisdom.

Chapter 8

BREATH OF HEAVEN

Windy clouds fill the air,
    Hands folded in prayer.
Paraclete! Paraclete!
Divine Dove, emerging out of a billowing cloud
    Blanket me like a shroud.
Holy Spirit, from above
    Anoint me with Your flaming love.

BROKEN PIECES

Broken pieces, we've all been broken,
    Broken pieces.
We come before God broken,
    Asking for help, needing help.
Not the way God intended it to be
    Just the way it is.
Holy God does His best to pick up and put back together the pieces of
    our lives
    Through faith and prayer.

CHRISTMAS TIME

Christmas passed when I was a boy
    Playing with my soldiers.
Christmas when I was a dad
    Handing out gifts.
Christmas spent alone
    Missing loved ones.
Always remember Christmas is Jesus's birthday.
Not ours.

EVIL KNOWS NO COLOR

Evil knows no color;
   It comes in every color.

GOD SEES EVERYTHING

God sees everything
 Including the seed that pushed through the earth
  To face the sunlight.
This sapling grew and sprouted leaves.
A tree whose branches swayed from the wind
 Casting a dark shadow on things to come.
One could hear birds nesting
 Until that day when a man cut it down
  And made a cross.
Perverting what God intended for a tree
 And His Son.

GOD'S WILL

God's will.
God's timing be done,
    Not ours!

I LOVE MYSELF MORE

One cannot see the devil Satan,
    Only his casualties.
Self-inflicted wounds hurt the most.
Don't give hate the power to destroy you.
Likewise, don't give grief the power to destroy you.

Love being reason enough to live,
    Is the lack of love reason enough to die?
No, I love myself more,
    For all the pain I've endured
        I love myself more.

JESUS, MY HERO

Once a Rabbi spoke about God and love
    All in the same breath,
        What he taught was that God is Love.

Jesus, the Son of God,
    Who hung bloody and dead on the cross,
        He is my hero.
The body of Christ was the seed
    God planted on earth to grow Christianity.

To live in the Light is never to die.
But to die in darkness is to lose your life.
Live and die in Christ.

LORD GOD ALMIGHTY

Lord God Almighty, I both love and fear You.
But it is out of love
      That I offer You my life.

RAPTURE

Jesus was a man of mystery,
    A man of deep sorrow.
Entombed one night in Jerusalem,
    Having supper at Emmaus another.
Where did he come from?
Where does he go?
What is it like in Paradise?
Nobody knows.
Jesus, a ghost that you can see.
Return O, Son of the Most High,
    Return and take us with you!

SPIRIT WITHIN

Spirit within,
I've loved You in whispers,
    Whispers in the wind
        On days sunny and dim.

Spirit within,
I've loved You in whispers,
    Whispers in the wind
        On nights spent alone or with family and friends.

Spirit within,
I've loved You in whispers,
    Whispers in the wind
        And inside where no one has been.

THE HOLY LAND

Sunlight upon a field of wildflowers overlooking the Sea of Galilee.
A silver star streaking across the night sky.
A man on his knees praying for peace in the Middle East.

THE MEANING OF LIFE

In regards to the meaning of life
Ignorant people say:
    That nobody knows.
Proud people say:
    They know.
But faithful people say:
    We believe.

THE SECOND COMING

Thinking about the centuries pass
    It is like watching a mighty river flow through time.
Time, a bridge to be crossed.

The Gospel of Christ
    Has been spoken down through the ages.
A holy calling,
    The voice of God
        Echoing the Second Coming!

TO YOU, I COUNT

Dear God,
I am but one grain of sand
   In a desert of sand,
      But to You, I count.

Chapter 9

HAVING FELT PAIN

Having felt pain and long-suffering
   Makes the joy of being in love
      All the sweeter.

IF SHE LOVED ME

If she loved me, I'd never feel so alone.
I'd have someone to share the day with
    And the holidays.
Every morning there would be a light in her eyes,
    An afternoon smile,
        And evening cuddles.

If she loved me, happiness would overflow.
The day wouldn't pass so fast,
    We could make time standstill
        If only for a moment.
If only she loved me.

IT'S QUIET NOW

It's quiet now, this evening.
Sun is silently setting, ending the daylight.
All thoughts still, just a calm peace, hover over me.
Gentle music is playing, and no one speaking.
Head clear.

Her face is gorgeous, dark eyes are warmly staring, and she has kissable
   pink lips.
A sweet, smile reaches me, insinuating everything.
Her long, black hair is ever so silky.
Midnight will be enchanting.

ONE-SIDED LOVE

One can't break my heart because it's already broken.
I'm looking for someone to help mend it.
One-sided love is not love
    It's misguided emotions.

THE YOUNG MAN THAT I WAS

The young man that I was is no more
    He's in the past.
The man that I am now is older, wiser.
The young man that I was is no more
    But his hair, his face did shine.

WAR MAKES NO SENSE

War makes no sense.
Why give Satan his way?
Rather than a country seeking nuclear weapons
    Seek to feed and shelter the poor
        And we, the people, would be a world better off.

Chapter 10

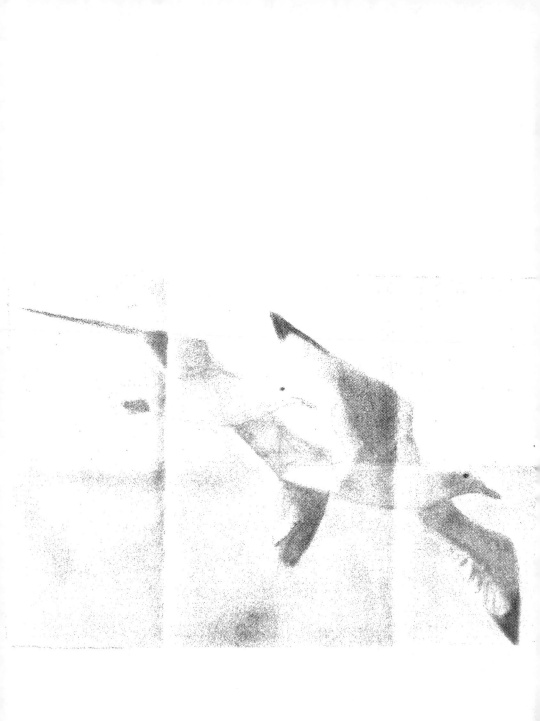

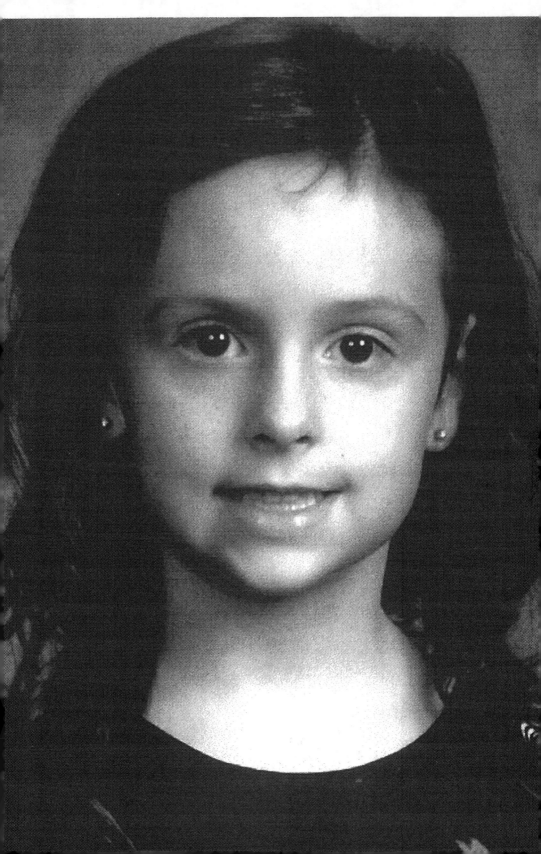

I'M ON MY WAY HOME

My time here near through
 Only a couple of things left to do
  Then I'll be coming home to You.
Flying with Godspeed
 I'm on my way home!

Bright skies await me.
Beauties never imagined.
Faith has saved me.
I am going to where my soul belongs,
 Where holiness abounds.
I'm on my way home!

Precious Light, Precious Light, I see You.
Celestial Energy of God, I feel You.
For all of eternity, I will be in love with Thee!
I'm on my way home!

Arms stretched out high like wings, my hands embracing the sky!
Looking up! Looking up!
Paradise is coming into view!
I'm on my way home!

Bright skies illuminate me.
Precious Light! Precious Light!
Arms stretched out high like wings, my hands embracing the sky!
I'm home!